Improving K-8 Reading Using Multiple Intelligences

by
Louisa Melton,
Winston Pickett,
and
Gail Sherer

ISBN 0-87367-648-3

Bloomington, Indiana

This fastback is sponsored by the
Tulsa Oklahoma Chapter of
Phi Delta Kappa International,
which made a generous contribution
toward publication costs.

Table of Contents

Introduction

From time to time intense debate has surfaced in the media over instructional strategies, such as whole language versus phonics and whole math versus traditional math. Most of the debate is cast in either-or terms. For example, whole language has been espoused by decrying the "evils" of phonics, without recognizing that the "whole" in whole language also includes appropriate instruction in phonics. But, too often, debate in the media emphasizes only simple solutions to complex problems.

Our goal in this fastback is to examine the learning process in reading, not with an eye to simple solutions, but with concern about problems and potential remedies. Within this framework we will discuss research on the brain and learning processes and suggest some ways to improve instruction for all children in grades K-8.

Education *is* changing. States now are funding prekindergarten programs in many areas because of renewed national emphasis on education. The scope and length of school programs is changing as society demands more from schools, not just in terms of education, but also in terms of child care. Business and industry are looking to the schools to produce future workers who are more capable, better educated, and willing to work cooperatively.

Within this complex milieu of demands and expectations, educators must understand a basic philosophy, which is that reading programs must be tailored to meet children's needs. We cannot expect children merely to adjust to the demands of a particular program.

Human developmental research indicates that there are basic developmental stages through which children commonly progress. There are universal, predictable sequences of growth and change in all domains of development: cognitive, social, emotional, and physical. And yet each child retains a certain uniqueness, a singular schedule and pattern of growth, which depends on his or her personality, lifestyle, and learning style. Experts agree that educators must structure teaching and learning to recognize both the universal and the individual and that students will learn most effectively when they are actively involved and invested in the education.

The ability to communicate is at the core of educational success. Reading is universally accepted as a basic tool of communication, essential in the modern world. Learning to read also is motivational for the young child. Kindergartners and first-graders come to school full of enthusiasm for learning to read. Why, then, do many students leave school with underdeveloped reading skills? Why do other students, capable readers, choose to read very little? Why do students' attitudes change? These are the questions that we will examine.

One direction for seeking answers is to accept that individuality is a key to success in reading, as in schooling in general. When educators embrace a philosophy of individuality, it becomes possible to address students' needs and interests as manifestations of their individuality. When teaching is structured around a philosophy of conformity, some students' needs are bound to be overlooked. Therefore, a central premise in examining the questions posed in the preceding paragraph is that teachers need to concern themselves with using instructional practices that match the learning styles and needs of students. For some teachers, this will mean abandoning "information transmission" strategies in favor of engaging students in "information transactions."

Background Factors

A number of factors need to be briefly set forth as background information, because they affect the development of reading skills. These factors include language development, early reading, cognitive ability, and learning styles.

Language Development and Early Reading

The precursor to learning to read is language development. Children begin developing language almost immediately after birth, initially using single words to label their world. By the time they are 18 months old, most children are using two-word and telegraphic speech involving nouns, verbs, and adjectives. And from the age of two years onward, language develops rapidly. Martin Braine's studies showed, for example, that one young child's two-word combinations grew from 14 to 2,500 in only seven months (Braine 1978).

In 1976, Walter Loban conducted an extensive longitudinal study of language development in school-age children. Loban's work recognized a firm relationship between oral language development and success in reading and writing. His study "provided the basis upon which our present day thinking about the integrated language arts curriculum rests" (Buckley 1992, p. 622). We now understand that by age four most children use grammatically correct sentences and begin to question why and how. This language foundation establishes the path on which the child will continue learning when he or she enters formal schooling. As a child's language skills develop, his or her cognitive abilities and personality traits also develop. And these traits affect the child's ability to learn and determine his or her learning style, or way of reacting to people, places, things, and events (Maxim 1993, p. 81).

Age-appropriate books are important in language development. Joanne Hendrick (1988) recommends the use of children's books and related activities to enhance language development at home and at school. George Maxim (1989) describes the role of literature in influencing positive social and cultural attitudes and suggests integrating multicultural education into the curriculum of the very young in order to enhance self-concept and cultural identity, to develop social skills, and to broaden the curriculum. Donna Norton, in *Through the Eyes of a Child* (1995), provides an extensive reading list of books that can promote social development of young children.

Lee Galda and Anthony Pellegrini (1985) emphasize the importance of encouraging children to respond to literature. Adults who interact with children through literature have an effect on how the words are preserved by the child, thus affecting the pleasure the child receives from the reading experience. Children's language, cognitive ability, personality, and social and moral development affect the way in which they respond to literature. Miriam Martinez and Nancy Roster, in a review of response research, state, "Researchers have identified numerous reader characteristics that influence response, including reader beliefs and expectations, reading ability, socioeconomic status, cultural background, cognitive development, sex, and personal style" (1991, p. 644).

Cognitive Ability and Learning Styles

Research involving cognitive ability and learning styles has received considerable emphasis in the education literature during the past 15 years. A number of theories and philosophies have been put forward, including multiple intelligences (MI) theory, brain-based learning theory, thinking styles, and learning styles.

Howard Gardner's *Frames of Mind* (1983) posited that learners gather knowledge through a variety of "intelligences," or ways of learning most effectively. Gardner's multiple intelligences include visual/spatial, logical/mathematical, body/kinesthetic, musical, interpersonal, intrapersonal, and verbal/linguistic. We will take these up in greater detail in the next section.

Brain-based learning theory posits that learning occurs only when the learner is an active participant in the acquisition of knowledge and the construction of meaning. Following are some of the beliefs that undergird brain-based learning theory:

- The brain is a parallel processor.
- Learning engages the entire physiology.

- The search for meaning is innate for the brain.
- Meaning is gathered by patterning information.
- Emotions are critical to patterning.
- The brain perceives and creates parts and wholes.
- Learning comes from a combination of focused and peripheral perceptions.
- Learning involves conscious and unconscious processes.
- The brain contains both spatial and rote memory.
- Understanding comes from both internal and external interaction.
- Learning comes about best when we are challenged but not threatened.

In essence teachers and parents do not "teach" a child to walk or talk; they merely provide opportunities for adaptations to an already operational process. This is a true example of transaction learning. Children learn best when learning is active, not passive. Brain-based learning principles challenge the basic assumptions of traditional education and help teachers to redevelop ideas concerning how to teach (Caine and Caine 1990).

Thinking styles theory suggests that there are certain ways of thinking that can be identified and described. Matching instruction to students' thinking styles can enhance learning. But the student who can flex, or use multiple styles, is more likely to be successful than students who can learn best in only one or two ways. The three branches of thinking styles include function, scope, and form (Sternberg 1990).

Function describes how an individual approaches skills. Students who depend on a "legislative" function engage in creating, formulating, imaging, and planning. Students who depend on an "executive" function engage in implementing and doing. And students who depend on a "judicial" function engage in judging, evaluating, and comparing.

Scope describes how an individual approaches problems: "internally" through independent work or "externally" through group work.

Form describes how an individual views problem solutions. Students who adopt a "monarchic" view see solutions as singular. Students who adopt a "hierarchic" view see multiple goals with various priorities. Students who adopt an "oligarchic" view see multiple goals of equal importance. And students who adopt an "anarchic" view take a random approach to seeking solutions to problems.

Learning styles theory posits that students learn best using one or more styles with which they are most comfortable. The most commonly identified styles are visual, auditory, and kinesthetic. Visual learners learn through watching, reading, and taking notes. Auditory learners learn through listening, verbal participation, and music. Kinesthetic learners learn through hands-on, active participation. Conventional, or traditional, teaching offers little recognition that students learn in highly individualistic ways. And learning to read is affected by how well instruction is matched to a student's learning style. Marie Carbo has provided numerous studies that define the shared roles of reading instruction and learning styles. The underlying theme of her research is that a student learns to read best when he or she is allowed to learn through his or her preferred learning style (Carbo 1980).

Brain-based learning, thinking styles, and learning styles theories are compatible with Gardner's multiple intelligences theory, which, in our view, offers an exemplary way of reorienting curriculum and instruction to effect more successful acquisition of reading skills in young students. Therefore, in the section that follows we take up MI theory as a thinking strategy for developing reading instruction, all the while cognizant of these other theories whose ideas also may assist in shaping success for all students.

Multiple Intelligences in Teaching and Learning

A reading program based on MI theory encourages students to learn to read in ways that make reading skills most meaningful to them.

Many of our traditional notions about reading instruction, learning, and human potential have been flawed and limited by single-dimension thinking. This is the conclusion of much of the research done during the 1980s and 1990s, particularly in the area of reading instruction.

For example, in the past we thought that an individual's intelligence was more or less fixed at birth and could be assessed through tests that resulted in a quantifiable "intelligence quotient," or IQ. However, the idea of "fixed potential" did not take into account the individual's background and experiences, factors that affect learning by enlarging or constricting the individual's capacity for knowledge acquisition. More recent research has shown that intelligence is far more flexible than we once thought. The present view — consistent with MI, brain-based learning, thinking styles, and learning styles theories — is that intelligence is multidimensional; there are many ways for individuals to learn because the brain/mind/body system is complex (Lazear 1992).

In *Frames of Mind* Gardner describes how the dependence on the scores from cognitive tests used to predict student success narrows the playing field of real-life accomplishments. He describes three students. One mastered navigation, another a foreign language, and a third computer programming for a music synthesizer. None of these high levels of attainment would be properly assessed by the cognitive tests typically used in schools. The gauge for intellectual success, in Gardner's view, should be changed to recognize students' personal strengths and interests and to enhance those intelligences. From Gardner's perspective, "it is not a question of how smart a student is, rather it is a question of how a student is smart" (Gardner 1983).

Gardner's MI theory posits several types of intelligence, as listed in the preceding section. That list can be amplified as follows:

- *Verbal/linguistic* intelligence centers on the use of words. Examples include reading, writing, analyzing, and organizing.
- *Logical/mathematical* intelligence concerns numbers and reasoning. Examples include strategies, games, science, and solving problems.
- *Spatial* intelligence involves pictures and images. Examples include diagrams, charts, and schemata.

- *Bodily* intelligence concerns the hands and body. Examples include kinesthetic activities, building models, and dramatizing events.
- *Musical* intelligence centers on using tones, rhymes, and rhythms. Examples include composing, singing, and learning in rhythmic ways.
- *Interpersonal* intelligence is the intelligence of social understanding. Examples include participation in group projects, clubs, and cooperative learning.
- *Intrapersonal* intelligence is the intelligence of self-knowledge. Examples include diaries, research, reflection, and individual projects.

To these seven original intelligences Gardner recently has begun to add naturalist and humorist intelligences.

The notion of teaching through multiple intelligences is refreshingly straightforward: Teachers should link instruction to all of the intelligences whenever possible for two reasons. First, no single mode of expression can fully convey the holistic sense of a subject. Most subjects are too complex to be reduced merely to the musical, for example, or to the linguistic. Second, because students learn in many different ways, subject matter should be presented in many different ways so that no student is left out. In this way every student's particular learning style or intelligence can be engaged.

Learning also cannot be disengaged from environment. Why does a student perform well and behave in one teacher's class but not in another's? The answer often lies in how teaching and learning are approached. So-called problem learners often are created by frustration. If the teacher's teaching style is mismatched to the student's learning style, the student may not be able to learn well and may become frustrated. Such frustration can diminish self-esteem and lead to misbehavior.

Using the MI framework in lesson planning involves asking questions related to each of the intelligences:

- How can I use the spoken or written word?
- How can I bring in numbers, calculations, logic, classifications, or critical thinking?
- How can I use visual aids, visualization, color, art, metaphor, or visual organizers?
- How can I bring in music or environmental sounds, or set key points in a rhythm or melody?
- How can I involve the whole body or hands in experience?
- How can I engage students in peer or cross-age sharing and cooperative learning?
- How can I evoke personal feelings or memories or give students choices?

An MI curriculum allows teaching to be multifaceted. Students make connections through their preferred learning methods. And, because many intelligence channels are used, students may acquire skills and attain greater comfort levels in intelligences of which they were previously unaware. In teaching through a curriculum based on multiple intelligences, learning becomes active and meaningful — and multidimensional. Similarly, the structure of an MI curriculum also encourages the teacher to expand his or her repertoire of teaching styles to meet the needs of a greater number of students.

Connecting MI Theory to Reading Instruction

One of the most important areas affected by a student's preferred intelligence(s) is learning to read. Each student learns to read best when allowed to learn through his or her own style. Middle school students who are poor or uninterested readers often have arrived at this point because they have not been allowed to learn and practice reading in a way that helps them to establish reading as an important part of life. Reading, like any skill, takes practice in order to become proficient. Poor readers often have many of the necessary basic skills, but they become uninterested in the material they are required to read; therefore their skills remain unpolished and reading becomes a chore, rather than a pleasure.

Poor readers frequently come from backgrounds that do not emphasize verbal skills and do not view reading as a valued skill. The poor reader often is a student who is peer-oriented (interpersonal intelligence) or highly attuned to spatial or bodily intelligences. This kind of learner needs to be allowed to move around while reading or practicing reading skills. By using an MI approach, teachers can reach these students as well as those who draw primarily on a verbal/linguistic intelligence.

MI also is helpful in working with students who speak English as a second language. Multiple input modes, using the various intelligences, will better assist struggling readers, particularly when the struggle is, first, to understand the new language. MI theory accentuates students' strengths and minimizes their weaknesses.

Conventional methods of instruction give little consideration to the individuality of each student and his or her preferred learning method. A curriculum designed around the intelligences can provide the flexibility to meet the different skills, needs, and abilities of today's students so they can become successful, active learners throughout life. Reading is not an isolated subject. It is a skill that is necessary for all teachers to incorporate in their lessons so that students will develop the techniques necessary to read for many different purposes.

A person's ability to read has a direct effect not only on the achievement of education goals but also on career choices and lifelong learning. Different reading patterns are established through practice. These patterns are applied in real-life situations for information, recreation, and literacy about the world in which we live. Reading patterns differ with reading purpose. Whether scanning for main points or studying for detail, practice of each reading pattern is required for mastery. Reading flexibility also is necessary to learn through a variety of teaching approaches. Silent reading and oral reading are skills that students must use daily in school and out. These skills must be incorporated in all subject areas of the school curriculum.

Students who are allowed to select their own material and are given a chance to read silently for a period each day develop reading skills more quickly than those who are given only required readings. The power to choose what one reads makes for the best reading program. Teachers can validate the importance of reading by also reading silently with their students during a daily free-reading period. Classrooms that are saturated with high-interest books significantly improve low-achieving students' attitudes toward school and reading. Conditions that promote an enthusiasm for reading include availability of books and magazines, adults and peers who model reading, sharing and discussing books, the involvement of both fiction and nonfiction books in subject instruction, and freedom of choice of reading material.

A multiple intelligences curriculum for enhancing the young child's interest in reading will include.

1. *Verbal/linguistic:*
- Story telling, using original, paraphrased, or verbatim renderings of familiar children's stories.
- Reading regular and big books silently and aloud.
- Writing books based on the theme of a told story, sometimes creating a new twist.
- Writing and drawing journals about books read or heard.

2. *Logical/mathematical:*

- Developing calendars of events in sequence as they happen in a story or book.
- Making categories for characters or objects in a story.
- Creating story maps and plot diagrams.

3. *Spatial:*

- Drawing or painting posters or pictures about stories read or heard.
- Creating a classroom mural to depict the plot of a story.
- Making a literature-rich environment with pictures, poems, and stories related to class reading.

4. *Bodily:*

- Creating plays or puppet shows that tell familiar stories or fairy tales.
- Developing flannel board stories created by the students.
- Making videotapes of peer performances.

5. *Musical:*

- Singing songs or making up rhymes or rap versions of stories read in class.
- Writing music to accompany an oral or choral reading.
- Developing an opera-style version of a book.

6. *Interpersonal:*

- Working in groups to produce a play based on a familiar story.

- Reading aloud using choral or round-robin techniques.
- Reading with a buddy; pairing younger and older students for reading aloud.

7. *Intrapersonal:*

- Choosing individual reading materials.
- Writing a journal of personal-choice reading activities.
- Participating in free-reading activities.

A truly integrated curriculum emphasizes connections among the intelligences, rather than delineating them as distinct processes. Thus a holistic approach provides opportunities for all students to become active readers in a variety of ways, to draw on their strengths, and to overcome their weaknesses by exploring new intelligences.

The use of narrative texts, rather than standard textbooks, can create more relevant, personal, and individualized learning. Narrative texts have special value to young students because they address the transitional reading stage that these students are experiencing. Often younger students have some of the necessary skills to read but lack a broad base of experience from which to develop meaning. Narrative texts use familiar story organization and offer needed description and details so that the student's interest will be held and his or her experiential background will be broadened.

Various forms of narratives can be used. Poetry, for example, offers language stimulation, humor, and new perspectives. Kinesthetic learners will be captivated —

and motivated — by plays or role-playing based on books and stories. Songs and rhymes tap musical intelligence. And so on. Traditional literature — myths, legends, ballads — can be used creatively in MI-based reading. Popular tales include those featuring Hercules, Jason and the Golden Fleece, Pecos Bill, and Paul Bunyan. Children also appreciate modern tales or fantasies, such as E.B. White's *Charlotte's Web* and Roald Dahl's *James and the Giant Peach*, which encourage students to expand their imaginations. But the same can be said for more realistic fiction, such as the novels by Beverly Cleary and Elaine Konigsburg.

Picture books offer easy reading for remedial or reluctant readers and can sharpen interest in learning to read more fluently. Picture books also can stimulate discussion or provide a basis for visual projects. Many picture books also offer students new perspectives and can help students see how to think creatively about various subjects. Good examples include Chris Van Allsburg's *The Polar Express* and Vera B. Williams' *A Chair for My Mother*.

Narrative need not be confined to the realms of fiction. Many high-quality nonfiction books for children use storylines and illustrations that make them highly interesting and motivating.

Both fiction and nonfiction narratives can lend themselves to the development of thematic units on many topics, not least among them cultural issues, such as diversity, gender equity, religion, and so forth. When planning a thematic unit, the teacher should remember:

- To identify themes based on student interests. An interest survey may be useful.
- To center thematic units around a variety of literature. For example, the theme of difference might be carried out using Eric Carles's *The Mixed-Up Chameleon*, Arnold Adoff's *All the Colors of the Race*, and Bernard Waber's *Ira Sleeps Over*. A friendship theme might draw on Russell Hoban's *Best Friends for Frances* and Kay Chorao's *Pearl and Oink*.
- To brainstorm about methods and activities, so that students feel invested in the learning and skills they will develop.
- To establish evaluation criteria "up front," so that students know what will be expected. Students should be involved in establishing evaluation criteria.

Some further examples of themes drawing on established children's books include:

- Family: Martha Alexander's *Nobody Asked Me If I Wanted a Babysitter*, Ezra Jack Keats' *Peter's Chair*, and Valerie Flournoy's *The Patchwork Quilt*.
- Work and Cooperation: Virginia Lee Burton's *Mike Mulligan and His Steam Shovel*, Eric Carle's *The Very Busy Spider*, Norma Klein's *Girls Can Be Anything*, and Margaret Mahy's *My Wonderful Aunt*.
- Attitudes and Peer Values: Paul Goble's *The Girl Who Loved Wild Horses*, F.N. Monjo's *The Drinking Gourd*, and Ina R. Friedman's *How My Parents Learned to Eat*.

Many ideas for active teaching and learning through the use of narrative texts are available in many commercial book series, but awareness of MI theory will allow the teacher to ensure that all of the students' learning needs are met.

Connecting Reading and Other Subjects

Children often feel that reading is boring. However, if a book is about a subject in which they are interested, such as history or science, they become more enthusiastic (Bristor 1994). This perception of the worth of reading points up the notion that reading instruction, to be effective, must be relevant. An MI approach to reading can readily incorporate other subjects, often treating them in much the same manner as thematic instruction. For example, students might read *The Magic School Bus Inside the Body* in the context of a science unit on the human body. Following are some ideas to illustrate the connections that might be made:

- *Verbal/linguistic:* Use the text as a vehicle for language arts study, such as finding main ideas, using context clues, noting punctuation, and so on. Have students write stories along the same lines as the book.
- *Logical/mathematical:* Ask students to explain the sequences used in the book. Where does the Magic School Bus travel and why? Have students explain the body systems in their own words.
- *Spatial:* Help students make internal body maps for the respiratory system and the digestive system.
- *Bodily:* Ask students to build a model of the respiratory system or act out the Magic School Bus' discoveries.

- *Musical:* Allow students to develop songs based on the book or to create rhymes that will help them remember the stopping points of the body systems.
- *Interpersonal:* Encourage students to work in small groups to create books or projects that tie together the science of the human body and related literature.
- *Intrapersonal:* Ask students to keep individual journals chronicling their discoveries as they read the *Magic School Bus Inside the Body* and other books.

Similar kinds of activities can be undertaken to relate reading to mathematics, history, art, music, and so on.

A particularly useful reading connection for current events (and a wide range of other subjects) is the newspaper. Many larger newspapers also participate in the Newspaper in Education (NIE) program, and connections to MI theory can be readily made.

Conclusion

The ability to read distinguishes humans from other animals. It opens the culture to new ideas and keeps us connected with the past. Today a person who cannot read is almost unemployable and is removed from many activities of our society. We cannot allow children to grow up with poor reading skills and habits, yet many students see little value in reading because there are so many other ways to get information. Yet even the most reluctant reader will acknowledge that they need the ability to read. Teachers must take the responsibility not merely to enhance each student's ability to read but also to engender in children a love of reading and a sense that reading is both pleasurable and productive.

The successful reading program is one in which a variety of techniques are incorporated. Such a program will include attention to many disciplines and incorporate both fiction and nonfiction. It will engage students through active participation in drama, art, musical and personal expression, cooperative learning, and individual writing. We suggest that these goals are a good fit with a multiple intelligences curriculum.

Children often see the obvious more clearly than do adults. In 1993 a middle school student wrote the following letter after studying MI theory and reflecting on his previous six years of schooling:

> Dear Board of Education,
>
> Recently I've been studying multiple intelligence theory, or M.I., in language arts. . . .
>
> I believe some children are geniuses but cannot show their intellectual abilities in linguistic and logical/mathematical, or standard, classes. Thus we must recognize these prodigies. To do this, we should organize the seven intelligences into the school systems. This will increase their chances of getting jobs and better grades. In conclusion. I have written this letter to inform you on M.I. Thank you for your time.
>
> Sincerely,
> C.H.

MI theory is relatively easy for even young children to grasp. Thus, in addition to presenting a way for teachers to think about teaching, it also offers a way for students to reflect on their own learning. This metacognitive aspect makes multiple intelligences all the more valuable as a teaching and learning theory with broad application in every area, not least of which is learning to read.

Resources

Armstrong, T. "Multiple Intelligences: Seven Ways to Approach Curriculum." *Educational Leadership* 51 (November 1994): 26-28.

Braine, M. "The Ontogeny of English Phrase Structure: The First Phase." In *Readings in Language Development*, edited by Lois Bloom. New York: John Wiley & Sons, 1978.

Bristor, V. "Combining Reading and Writing with Science to Enhance Content Area, Achievement, and Attitudes." *Reading Horizons* 35, no. 1 (1994): 31-43.

Buckley, M. "Focus on Research: We Listen a Book a Day; We Speak a Book a Week: Learning from Walter Loban." *Language Arts* 69 (December 1992): 622-26.

Caine, M R., and Caine, G. "Understanding a Brain-Based Approach to Learning and Teaching." *Educational Leadership* 48 (1990): 66-70.

Carbo, M. "Reading Style: Diagnosis, Evaluation, Prescription." *Academic Therapy* 16 (September 1980): 45-52.

Carbo, M. "Five Schools Try Reading Styles Programs." *Early Years* 15 (August/September 1984): 52-61.

Carbo, M. "You Can Identify Reading Styles. . . and Then Design a Super Reading Program." *Early Years* 15 (April 1984): 80-83.

Dunn, R. "Rita Dunn Answers Questions on Learning Styles." *Educational Leadership* (October 1990): 15-18.

Galda, Lee, and Pellegrini, Anthony D., eds. *Play, Language, and Stories: The Development of Children's Literate Behavior*. Norwood, N.J.: Ablex, 1985.

Gardner, H. *Frames of Mind*. New York: Basic Books, 1983.

Gray, J., and Veins, J. "The Theory of Multiple Intelligences: Understanding Cognitive Diversity in Schools." *Phi Kappa Phi Journal* 74 (Winter 1994): 22-25.

Hendrick, J. *The Whole Child*. 4th ed. New York: Merrill/Macmillan, 1988.

Hough; D., and Donlan, D. "Achieving Independent Student Responses Through Integrated Instruction." *Middle School Journal* 25 (May 1994): 22-25.

Lazear, D. *Teaching for Multiple Intelligences*. Fastback 342. Bloomington, Ind.: Phi Delta Kappa Educational Foundation, 1992.

Leland, C., and Fitzpatrick, R. "Cross-Age Interaction Builds Enthusiasm for Reading and Writing." *Reading Teacher* 47 (1994): 292-301.

Martinez, M., and Roster, N. "Children's Responses to Literature." In *Handbook of Research on Teaching of the English Language Arts*, edited by James Flood, Julie M. Jensen, Diane Lapp, and James R. Squire. New York: Macmillan, 1991.

Maxim, George W. *The Very Young: Guiding Children from Infancy Through the Early Years*. Columbus, Ohio: Merrill, 1989.

Maxim, G. T*he Very Young: Guiding Children from Infancy Through the Early Years*. New York: Merrill/Macmillan, 1993.

Norton, D. *Through the Eyes of a Child*. 4th ed. Upper Saddle River, N.J.: Merrill/Prentice-Hall, 1995.

Moffett, J., and Wagner, B. " Student-Centered Reading Activities." *English Journal* 80 (1991): 70-74.

Oliver, P. *Developing the Curriculum.* New York: HarperCollins, 1992.

O'Neil, J. "Making Sense of Style." *Educational Leadership* (October 1990): 4-9.

Poindexter, C. "Applying Effective Reading Techniques in Content Area Classes." *Reading Horizons* 35, no. 3 (1995): 245-49.

Smith, J., and Herring, J. "Drama in the Middle Level Classroom: Bringing Content to Life." *Middle School Journal* 26 (September 1994): 30-36.

Sternberg, R.J. "Thinking Styles: Keys to Understanding Student Performance." *Phi Delta Kappan* 71 (January 1990): 366-71.

Sternberg, R.; Okagaki, L.; and Jackson, A. "Practical Intelligence for Success in School." *Educational Leadership* 48 (September 1990): 35-39.

Zientarski, D., and Pottorff, D. "Reading Aloud to Low Achieving Secondary Students." *Reading Horizons* 35, no. 1 (1994): 45-51.